OFF THE FIELD
Carving Your Own Path To Find Your
Best Self

by China McCarney

i

For My Family John, Barb, Loretta, Jennie and Nash. For My Friends. Those that have come and those that have gone. Those that I've lost and those that I've not yet found.

Contents

Introduction

Purpose.
A single word that at first glance seems simple enough.

We all have a vague definition about what purpose means. We all have an idea as to what our purpose is. As you read these first few sentences you are probably starting to think about your purpose.

How clear are those thoughts?

Where did those thoughts come from?

The truth is, until you start to think about questions like these you may find yourself going through the motions in life. You may find yourself going through the same routine year after year until one day you realize you have arrived at a destination that you really had nothing to do with. Step after step you listened to people and what they thought was best for you, or what they thought you should do.

You realize: **Your purpose isn't yours.**

Unfortunately, this happens much more often than it should. Stereotypes, media portrayals and the way it "should be" all go into how we view the world and how we mold ourselves. This, of course, is not all bad. There are a number of great examples both past and present on how to be successful, how to be a great person and how to contribute to the world. These examples, portrayals and outside influences should be contributing factors to deciding your purpose and your passion. However, they should not be the number one determining factor; **that factor should come from within.**

My purpose in writing this book is not to preach nor share any sort of "one size fits all" approach to life. It is simply to share my experiences as an athlete and the way a deteriorating desire to play athletics **helped me look within to find my purpose and my passion.** I feel the lessons I have learned in this first chapter of my life can help others who are going through the same experiences. It may help you take a look inside of yourself to see what makes you tick.

This is not a book for just athletes. It is written through the eyes of an athlete for any human being who has struggled. We are all on a team of some sort. We all compete. We all desire to improve. We all make mistakes or come up short on occasion. We all have goals. We all have daily battles. Whether an athlete or not, we are all in this together and the more we share and lift each other up the better our world and society will be.

Through my ups, downs, struggles and hardships the desire to improve and to find purpose grew. I realized that there is something extremely powerful when it comes to struggles and hardships. Your struggles and hardships can be huge blessings if you look at them the right way and with the right perspective.

There are two ways to look at negative occurrences in your life. You can look to other

people and outside influences on what you should feel, say or do about them. Or you can look within at how YOU really feel, what positives can be taken out of the situation and decide to use it as fuel and as a positive.

This simple fact about struggles is what led me to the epiphany of what my true passion and purpose is at this stage of my life. I will dive into my struggles in detail in later chapters and explain how I believe my worst struggles are my biggest blessings. As I stated, I am an athlete and will use my athletic experiences to relate to everyday life. However, it was my struggles away from athletics that began to force my focus away from the world and back on myself. It was that process that began to show me what the problem was really all about.

I was not pursuing my passion. I was not committed to my purpose. My struggles were OFF THE FIELD and I would learn that my passion and purpose lie there too.

My goal with this book is to share my experiences and how they have led me to what I currently do: **Wake up on a daily basis and pursue my**

passion. Not a passion that was laid out for me, or what people thought I should do, a passion that developed inside of me silently while I was on the field. A passion that kept quiet and slowly grew a voice as the on-field desire was breaking down. A passion that I would not see until I took the time to look within for what my **true purpose** was.

This is the theme of this book, to **take it upon yourself to decide how you feel, to decide how things will affect you and to decide what your passion and purpose is.**

Commit to you. Carve your path. Find your best self.

Chapter 1
Self Discipline

Self discipline is the key to success. However far you want to go, whatever level of success you want to achieve, it all falls on you. Your view of yourself. Your views of your circumstances. Your ability to be disciplined and to do whatever it takes to accomplish your goals. **At the end of the day you really only have one person to answer to: yourself.**

Personal Experience
This is a powerful lesson to learn. It was taught to me by a student I was training during the off-season of Major League Baseball. The athlete I was training had accomplished pretty much everything to the outside eyes. He was an All Star, a World Series Champion and had been on the

mound to record the last out of the World Series before he and his teammates celebrated together in the middle of the field. He has enough money to last him many lifetimes and yet he and I shared one of the most powerful conversations I have had to this point in my life. It was a conversation about improving as a person and holding yourself accountable.

The subject of Self Discipline came up and his whole demeanor changed. He was passionate, energetic and spoke with a fire I hadn't seen from him up to this point. "Everything in life comes down to Self Discipline", he said. At first, I had objections in my head. Outside influences, circumstances, upbringing, all of these excuses rushed through my brain as they would rush through the majority of our heads. However, as I thought more and more about his words, and he and I spoke more about the subject, I realized he had helped me reach an epiphany. Self Discipline can be the foundation to living our best life and we really are in control of far more than we realize.

If we go through the day with Self Discipline at the forefront of our minds we will make far more productive decisions and be far more successful.

Not only that, the outside influences that we can not control will not hold us prisoner as they so often do.

Far too many times we let variables that we can not control affect us more than we should. We let a negative occurrence influence our next step for hours, days, months and more frightening, sometimes years. If we stop that cycle from the beginning and realize **we are in control of our reaction to all situations,** we can be far more productive, positive and successful just by being disciplined within ourselves.

Easier said than done right? We will get much more into struggles, shortfalls and mistakes later in the book but it is important to realize that we can control much more than we think with our initial outlook on situations and circumstances. It is like anything else, **you have to practice and work on being Self Disciplined and it will start becoming normal.**

One of the first steps with Self Discipline is us getting comfortable with holding ourselves accountable. This is an extremely difficult practice to put into play because the majority of us are not used to this.

It is not necessarily our fault, it is the way we have been trained over time and the way our society has been heading for years. **Each generation is becoming more and more of a finger pointing generation.** If something goes wrong we search for who we can blame. We do this because we believe there is no possible way that anything could be our fault.

We see finger pointing all over the place now with news broadcasts, movie portrayals and especially social media. We see this in professional athletics constantly and we see this with parents and children as well.

If a child makes a mistake or gets into trouble the first thing parents try to do is to find out who caused their child to make a mistake. They struggle to accept the fact that either their child chose to do something wrong, or even worse, that their parenting hadn't prepared their child for a certain situation. They point the finger, the child learns to point the finger and so on and so on.

This has become an increasingly common practice in our society and it needs to be addressed. **The solution starts with individuals making their own decisions, accepting their actions and holding themselves accountable for what those actions and decisions result in.** Again, this is not easy.

However, a common theme in this book is that **success is not easy and you have to work for anything you want to achieve or accomplish.**

You have to re-lay the foundation and rewire yourself to instinctually look within before looking outward when a negative situation occurs. You have to believe in your ability to make the right decisions. When something goes wrong, you have to first look at yourself and at what you could have done better and where you can adjust. That takes ultimate Self Discipline. **Ultimate Self Discipline is looking in the mirror when something goes wrong and accepting it. Once we've accepted responsibility, we can learn from the situation and make an adjustment to give ourselves a better chance to succeed the next time a similar situation arises.**

These are the broad strokes with Self Discipline. Now that a foundation has been laid let's look at it more closely.

What does it look like to me?

What are some experiences I have had with positive and negative Self Discipline?

What can it look like in your life?

Self Discipline is defined as the ability to control one's feelings and overcome one's weaknesses; the ability to pursue what one thinks is right despite temptations to abandon it. To me, this means Self Discipline is making small decisions every day to improve yourself to get closer to what you are trying to achieve.

The reason a majority of us do not stick to a program or achieve our long term goal is because we try to achieve it quickly. We do something too extreme. That is not what Self Discipline is about. Self Discipline is about holding yourself accountable everyday and making positive adjustments when needed. That is the recipe for long term success -- Training yourself over a long period of time until being disciplined and being successful is your norm.

SELF DISCIPLINE IS A LIFESTYLE.

We have all seen a version of this in our lives at some point. For me as an athlete, I saw this often in others especially as I moved higher and higher throughout the game of baseball. Some guys just had a different edge about them and a different commitment level to their craft. I am sure you have all seen people like this in your life. Someone who is more committed at the office. Someone who gets their workouts in no matter what. Someone who can say no to that "one more" beer that will send them over the top.

We have all seen these examples and some of us are probably implementing some of these steps in our own life.

The question is:

How do we implement this on a daily basis and maintain these actions of Self Discipline long term?

We have to learn from our experiences both past and present and implement positive adjustments.

Personal Experience

I want to share one positive experience and one negative experience I have had with examples of Self Discipline. I will share the negative experience first so we can end on a happy note. When I was a Junior in college I was playing Division I baseball. I had everything going for me. I was projected to get drafted, make a lot of money and at the beginning of the season everything was positive. I was working as hard as I could to achieve my goal of being a professional athlete.

The beginning of that season was like a dream. I was putting on a Division I uniform with CSUN across the chest and competing against some of the best schools in the country that I had grown up watching. I earned the honor and the right to start opening day against Pepperdine University in Malibu, CA in 2009. I can almost still smell the air at one of the most beautiful settings in college baseball overlooking the Pacific Ocean. The nerves I felt that day were like none other I had ever felt. They were normal nerves about competing but they were also due to the fact that I was going to be on the mound on opening day in Division I Baseball.

It was a huge accomplishment and earlier that week I informed my dad I would be getting the ball in the first game. He and I had a choked up moment together on the phone. All of the hours practicing together on the back fields of Sierra Pony Baseball in Acton, CA had paid off. All of the money for showcases and constant travel ball had all come to a head and he and I could share in a moment that many fathers and sons dream about.

The game on that opening Friday night went amazing. I left the game after pitching 7 strong innings, our team was up 2-1 and in a position to beat the then ranked number 11 team in the country. Unfortunately, they would hit back to back home runs in the bottom of the ninth inning to beat us but the experience is cemented in my mind as one of my favorite of all time.

The season was off and running and it was getting exciting. I started 5 or 6 straight Friday night games and pitched well in all but one of them. The professional scout attention got stronger and stronger every week and all I needed to do was stay healthy, work hard, stay focused and I would get my desired result. At least that is what I thought I had to do, but as positive as the beginning of that season was, I had no idea the hardships and struggles that were to come.

Shortly after the beginning of that season the head coach decided to take me out of a starting role on the team. I was blindsided by his decision that I could not control. I immediately lost sight of my Self Discipline and my training. I let his decision get me into such a negative outlook that I stopped training as hard as I had been and it affected my entire season and really my entire career. It was my choice to view the situation as a complete negative. I could have looked at it as a challenge to push harder and stay disciplined, and I didn't. To me, that is flat out WEAK!

One side note to this story that could shed light on the ultimate inner approach we are trying to achieve is that the coach of that team had, and has, a track record of making poor decisions and negatively affecting player's careers. Anyone who was around the situation, especially professional scouts, informed me that there was nothing I could have done and it was unfortunate the position I was put in.

This is likely true and I could easily accept everyone's words that is wasn't my fault but that would be wrong. The coach obviously thought he was doing right and I could have done more. Maybe the results would not have been changed but I know I could have worked harder and had a better approach. The negative reaction was on me and I could have had better Self Discipline.

Ok. Now a positive story about Self Discipline. This is going to feel like such a simple story but it changed my life literally overnight.

I was just entering the "real world" of working in business instead of playing a game for a living and our company had a clinic going on one day. We had a guest speaker at the clinic named Tim Dixon of thementallocker.com who gave a brief 5-10 minute speech. The impact he would have on me that day is one I will never forget. I had known Tim for some time but we were still in the infant stages of our friendship and business relationship. I had not heard him speak up to this point. He spoke about the relationship with practice, being a predator, and a simple concept about Amateur vs. Professional. I am not going to steal his words and share everything he said but in short the Amateur vs. Professional concept was about everyday decisions we make and are we being an Amateur or a Professional.

That night I arrived home late. I was exhausted from the day. Speaking and teaching the kids, doing the Long Toss demonstration and just being in the sun for hours had taken it out of me. I was filthy with sweat from the day and had an inner debate while standing at the foot of my bed. I wanted to go straight to sleep. I did not want to shower and take care of any of the other chores I had to do. Then, I heard a voice inside my head. We all have them at times in many different tones and cadences, but this one was clear and it was Mr. Dixon.

"Amateur vs. Professional."

Amateur would have been hopping into bed a sweaty mess and not worrying about any of the other chores. That night, however, I made the professional choice to take a shower and get the chores done that needed to be done. A simple choice but so powerful for me and my journey.

It was Self Discipline at its finest. These are the little choices I spoke of before. It is the difference between being elite and being average. You can start laying the framework for you to be a more Self Disciplined person. **The little choices start to add up and you begin rewiring yourself to get things done instead of putting them off.** Procrastination goes away and you feel so powerful and accomplished in the instances that you can show Self Discipline.

This is what Self Discipline can look like in your life. You can start making these little choices that will start to add up. You will start to see the lasting effects of your improved habits and your life conditions will improve. You will start to feel more passion about your everyday routine. If you don't, you will realize that your everyday routine isn't your passion or your purpose. You will use that new found Self Discipline to pursue your passion.

Again, everything in this book is simple. It all boils down to inward reflection and inward responsibility to achieve what it is that you want to achieve. It is about you listening to yourself, and being the best you, so that you can reach your true potential. In doing this, you and everyone around you will benefit. It is about taking the focus off of the outside world and really figuring out what makes you go, where your desire lies and what your purpose is on this earth.

We are all capable of far more than we realize. When we unshackle ourselves from outward expectations and commit to our passion, the possibilities are endless.

Chapter 1 Take Away

- **Everything comes back to SELF DISCIPLINE**

- **Look within and EMPOWER YOURSELF. It is your choice on how you react to situations and circumstances**

- **PRACTICE SELF DISCIPLINE daily and it becomes easier just like anything else**

- **"PRACTICE MAKES PERFECT" is wrong. PERFECT IS UNATTAINABLE; "PRACTICE CREATES IMPROVEMENT"**

- **HOLD YOURSELF ACCOUNTABLE. Your Self Disciplined choices add up over time and begin to become your norm**

- **SELF DISCIPLINE IS A LIFESTYLE**

Chapter 2
Commitment from Within

The main themes in this book all come down to some form of commitment. You have to be fully committed to what you are doing if you truly want to reach the full potential of that situation.

The most pure form of commitment is Commitment From Within.

Commitment From Within means you are so committed to your passion and your purpose that your actions, words and thoughts all align. This is impossible to achieve when outside influences and outside expectations are impacting and manipulating you as a whole.

This point hits a very particular nerve with me. I had always thought that my commitment at a given time was coming from within myself and was directed at a goal that I had. This is how most of us feel.

Of course what we are doing and what we are committed to is coming from within us, right? Not always.

We can be committed to going down a path that we have nothing to do with. We are simply following a path of which we did not lay a single brick to help form.

I grew up in an athletic family. We watched sports, we based our schedules around games and our color coordinations were all based on our favorite teams. It was what we did. Sports ruled all. This should sound familiar to everyone and I am not talking about the theme of sports necessarily.

We all grow up in a family that has an identity of some sort. Some families are based strictly around religion. Some families are based strictly around academics and going to the finest institutions. Hopefully there is a balance of many things. The reality is that this is not the case the majority of the time. Certain things make certain people tick and they base a lot of their life around that because it is comfortable and that is their passion. Believe me, I am not saying anything is wrong with this but it can influence family members and friends in a way that may not even be recognized on the surface.

Let's dive deeper into this point. This point is so important in relation to realizing what our true passion is and what our true purpose is. Parents influence children. Spouses influence spouses. Friends influence friends. Media and television influence everyone to a certain extent. This is a normal part of life and part of how we become who we are.

We are the sum of all of our decisions and actions.

We are also the sum of all of the things we have been told to do, believe in and pursue. What happens when we don't agree with something but go along with it anyway because of love or for the fear of being "different"? This is the million dollar epiphany.

Little decisions to quiet your inner voice because of fear or blind love can slowly start to eliminate your true identity. You are not committing to anything from within because you are letting the outside world, the people close to you or your peers dictate your beliefs, passions and drive. This happens constantly and most people do not even realize it is happening in their own life because it is the norm in our society.

"I can't be different."

"I don't want to make anyone mad."

"Well they believe this and they are above me in stature so I must follow suit."

These are all the doubting thoughts in our heads that drive us away from our inner self. They drive us away from committing to what our passion is and what we really want to do. The second we realize this and start to change our outlook is the second we start to rebuild our true identity that we have quieted for so long.

Personal Experience

*I am a perfect example of this. Actually, I **was** a perfect example of this. I could have deleted that first sentence and just wrote "I was" but I left it because it proves the point that I am making. I wrote I <u>am</u>, but this isn't true. I <u>was</u> an example of this for all the years I played the sport of baseball after the passion and desire to play had left me. However, I am no longer a prisoner of the outside world or of outside expectations. Yes, I still struggle and still come up short but I wake up on a daily basis pursuing my passion and, from within, I feel I am committed to my purpose.*

I want to share my experience because I feel it will help many people do a gut check on themselves. It will help them realize whether or not they are committed to a goal from within.

As I touched on before I played baseball my entire life. Growing up and going through the levels I received many awards and was touted a "top prospect" by many publications. Naturally I kept on pursuing the dream of becoming a professional athlete because it was what I was told to do. College and professional scouts were in constant contact about where to play, what to do and how to be the best in their eyes.

My family and friends in my tiny hometown were excited at the idea of someone from Agua Dulce, CA making it to the professional ranks and putting the town "on the map". It was all on my shoulders and I thought that it was what I was meant to do. What I did not realize at the time was that the only reason I felt playing baseball was what I was meant to do was because of the outside noise. My inner voice and inner commitment was muted because I did not want to let everyone down. I did not want to be different and I wanted the approval of the people that loved me and that I loved.

This next sentence may seem like an incredibly egotistical thing to say but I will explain why it is anything but. I was blessed and cursed with Major League talent to play the game of baseball. When someone has an extreme talent, people think that it is what they are meant to do. This is an especially important point for parents. Just because your kids are good at something does not mean it is what they want to do. It may be what you want them to do but it may not be their desire or their passion.

*My dad is my best friend. He has been my biggest supporter in life and to this day he remains my closest contact and my exclusive confidant. He and I have had a number of conversations about this subject and he opened his eyes and mine about how the journey of my athletic career kind of blinded us away from my true passion. As a father he saw the talent I had and knew I had opportunities in the sport that many others did not. He encouraged me to continue to play and pursue opportunities just as many parents would. When I decided to retire from the game I was worried most about telling him because I knew it would hurt him. This comes back to the point about the outer versus inner commitment. **I was doing a disservice to my entire life by continuing to pursue a goal that wasn't mine from within.***

When I finally did retire and began to pursue my passion Off The Field my dad could not have been more supportive and proud. He saw the life in me. He saw the energy in me. He saw the passion I woke up with everyday. He saw the inner commitment oozing out of me on a daily basis. I was so worried about how the decision to walk away from my athletic playing career would affect others that I blinded myself to how great it would be to commit to me; commit to my inner passion.

This is the lesson here. **The people who are your true supporters, and are around you for the right reasons, want to see you be you**. They want to see you waking up each day and committed to something that means something to you. If they don't then they are not around you for the right reasons and they will eliminate themselves from your life or you will eliminate them from yours.

When you realize what it feels like to commit to something from within and attack it with self discipline, you will feel a new level of fulfillment in life that can not be matched.

Ask yourself if you are waking up each day with a clear purpose or passion?

Are you committed from within to do whatever it takes to achieve that passion or that purpose?

It is your choice. Remember we are all capable of far more than we know and when you commit, plan and attack with passion there are no shackles anymore.

YOU CONTROL YOUR DESTINY

Chapter 2 Take Away

- **What are you committed to?**

- **Where does your commitment come from?**

- **COMMIT to the PASSION and PURPOSE you have WITHIN YOURSELF.**

- **We are the SUM of all of our DECISIONS and ACTIONS.**

- **DO NOT quiet your inner voice. LISTEN to it. EMBRACE it. FEED OFF of it.**

- **COMMIT TO YOU**

Off The Field: Carving Your Own Path To Find Your Best Self

Chapter 3
Inner Competition and Inner Scoreboard

A constant desire in life for most people is the desire to compete. On some level we all want to compete and we all want to win. At times we all compare ourselves to someone or something. We do this to check on ourselves. We do this because we want results.

Results are great and they are the barometer on which we judge ourselves and judge others. However, results are not what we should focus on. **We must focus on the process of being Self Disciplined and pursuing our passion on a daily basis to achieve our end goal**. Again, it is a lifestyle and not a quick fix or instant success. It is the process of a step by step approach and keeping track of your positive and negative outcomes.

If you think back over the course of your life, and as I look back on mine, the things that are cherished the most are the things that we worked toward and accomplished. Those are our most satisfying moments. Why? Because it took commitment, it wasn't easy and the journey meant as much as the end result.

That is where true fulfillment comes from. That is where we truly feel our purpose and our worth. It is the step by step discipline and commitment that gets us to where we want to be. If you are truly committed to the process of the journey, to get to the desired result, you and everyone around you are benefitting from your pursuit and your passion.

So how do we know if we are committing to the process?

How do we know if we are improving our Self Discipline?

How do we know if we are pursuing our passion?

It is what I like to call Inner Competition and the Inner Scoreboard.

Let's cover the Inner Scoreboard first because it will be the barometer on how your Inner Competition is progressing.

The Inner Scoreboard is YOUR honest assessment of yourself. Your level of commitment to your passion. Your level of Self Discipline on a given day. Your level of your commitment to your life. If we really think about it we are the best judges of ourselves. We do not need the outside world to tell us if we are doing well or not. We know inside of ourselves if we are giving 100% effort and are working toward a true passion and purpose or not.

A simple exercise to do is as follows:
At the end of each day look back and give your own honest assessment of yourself.

Did I wake up and pursue my passion?

Did I feel 100% committed to the tasks I was doing?

Were those tasks meaningful and helping me get closer to achieving my ultimate goal?

Did I make disciplined decisions today?

As you begin to do this you will start to weigh your positives versus your negatives and you will have your Inner Scoreboard. The more you begin to do this the more it will be at the front of your mind throughout the day. The more your Inner Scoreboard is at the front of your mind the more it will start to influence your decisions more positively. This is where the Inner Competition comes in.

The more you begin utilizing the Inner Scoreboard the more you will be aware of your Inner Competition everyday in the present moment.

A situation will come up in your life just like it has everyday up to this point. It will give you the opportunity where you can make a positive productive choice or a normal mediocre choice. If you are aware of the Inner Competition you will compete with yourself. You will begin wanting your disciplined and committed self to defeat your normal mediocre self.

The more Inner Competitions you win the more fulfilled and successful you will become.

I want to keep sharing my experiences in my life to try and help bring clarity to these concepts. I want to make it clear that no matter what point you are at in your life there is improvement that can be made. You can commit more. You can more fully pursue your passion. You can improve your Self Discipline. This can be a huge overhaul for you or minor adjustments in your life. The key is that you are honest with yourself about how well you are doing on the Inner Scoreboard and if the competitions you are pursuing are truly your passion. That is the only way to see the true adjustments that need to be made and the only way to start improving.

I had a pivotal moment when I was 25 years old.

Personal Experience
I had been playing baseball for 20 years and had accomplished a great deal. I liked the results on my Inner Scoreboard and I felt as if I was winning

most Inner Competitions. I had no idea that my Inner Competitions and my Inner Scoreboard had nothing to do with what I was passionate about. I was blinded by the routine. I was blinded by the outside voices and accolades telling me I was doing great. Of course at that point I did not know these concepts but looking back and analyzing my mental state I know I felt this way at the time.

I was in Pittsburgh, Pennsylvania for Spring Training for Independent Professional Baseball. I had decided to give it one last run at pursuing an on the field professional baseball career. I had used the last 9 months to prepare my body, arm and mind to be the best that I could be. I had really given all 25 years of my life to preparation for that season but I was extremely focused and narrow minded during those particular 9 months of preparation.

I had driven from Los Angeles, CA to Pittsburgh, PA with my step mom Barb. It was a fun trip that took four full days of driving and I could feel the excitement and anticipation growing as we got closer and closer to our destination. This was another moment like the Opening Day start in Division I baseball where everything seemed like it was going to come together and I was going to achieve everything that everyone had always wanted me to achieve.

I had no idea what was about to happen when we finally arrived in Pittsburgh and I was not prepared for what the weeks of Spring Training would bring. I had no idea that the single most important event in my life was about to occur.

I threw my first bullpen a couple of days into Spring Training and immediately I could tell that something was not right with my arm. I could feel numbness in two of my fingers and I felt as if I had never thrown a baseball in my entire life. I did not know for sure but I felt like my velocity was significantly down. The next day all of these things would be confirmed. My numbers were nowhere near what they had been in the past and the team brought in a doctor to test me out and see what the issue was. He did one test in the clubhouse and informed me that I was done for the year. I had a genetic injury in my elbow that needed to be operated on right away. It was something I could not have controlled nor prepared for.

I was shocked. I was angry. I was upset.

A flood of emotions that I couldn't explain. All of the work, effort, travel and money gone in the first week that I was there.

A curse? No.

Probably the single most ultimate blessing in my life up until this point.

I had to have surgery on my arm shortly after finding out my season was over. The coming months would be a lot of sitting around in a sling and being without teammates or influences. It would be a time without a set schedule. I no longer had to eat, sleep, drink baseball. I had no idea that the coming months would give me a chance to analyze my goals, passion, desire, purpose and Inner Scoreboard.

What I would realize would change my life forever and finally give me a chance to discover that my true passion was Off The Field.

As recovery progressed and I began thinking about rehabbing my arm to play again, I had no passion or desire to get back to playing. I realized that I wanted to pursue business. I had always known this on some level on the inside but as I said before my inner voice and desires had been muted. I had not paid attention to what I truly wanted. I wanted to help people. I wanted to share all of my stories with as many people as I could to see if it would help them at all. I had realized that I had been Pursuing a Passion and a goal that wasn't mine. I had realized that I had been looking at a fake Inner Scoreboard and that it was not my score but everyone else's.

This may sound like a negative realization but to me it is the exact opposite. I feel so fortunate that I realized my true passion and decided to pursue it. I began to realize that many people may never give themselves a chance to look at their true self. I wanted to help in some way and that is what I am hoping to do in writing this book. It starts with Purpose and Passion. It continues with setting a plan and having Self Discipline. It is then monitored with Inner Competitions and an Inner Scoreboard.

It took the "catastrophic event" of my arm injury to give me a chance to gain perspective on my path and my life.

What if you never have an event like that occur and you go through the motions your entire life?

What if you never have a chance to wake up each day and pursue your passions?

We do not have to worry about questions like these. We are giving ourselves the chance to take a look inside of ourselves and hang up the Inner Scoreboard to monitor our progress. Only we can give a true assessment of ourself. **We have to be completely honest in our assessment of ourselves to achieve the maximum results and to truly be our best.**

I want to bring up another example from Tim Dixon because it adds tremendous value to what we are talking about here. I have heard Mr. Dixon speak many times now and one theme he speaks about often is being the best version of yourself. That is exactly what Inner Competition and the Inner Scoreboard looks like to me.

The outside world disappears and we have one person to compare ourselves to, the best version of OURSELF. Only we as individuals know what that looks like for us and that is what we need to strive for. That is really what is best for us and best for the world as a whole.

Can you imagine if everyone was truly committed to being the best version of themselves? Sounds like heaven on earth to me.

The good news is that by reading this book we are getting a blueprint of how to put a plan in motion to achieve this for ourselves. Yes, I am including myself in there because this is a non-stop battle for EVERYONE, every single day, until we are no longer on this earth.

We have a chance every single day to win the Inner Competition and like the results on the Inner Scoreboard. We have a chance every day to be as Mr. Dixon says, "The best version of ourselves!"

Chapter 3 Take Away

- **SUCCESS is a PROCESS. There is NO QUICK FIX**

- **ASSESS YOURSELF. Be HONEST with YOURSELF**

- **INNER SCOREBOARD is the way to monitor your PROGRESS**

- **INNER SCOREBOARD only works if you are truly HONEST with YOURSELF**

- **INNER COMPETITION is the ultimate battle between YOU and the BEST YOU**

- **COMPETE every day with the BEST YOU**

- *"BE THE BEST VERSION OF YOURSELF"* - **Tim Dixon**

Off The Field: Carving Your Own Path To Find Your Best Self

Chapter 4
Accepting Shortfalls and Mistakes

We have touched on discipline, passion, purpose and a lot of other golden words that are positive. These words sound easy to achieve.

"I am going to wake up everyday and be the best version of myself."

"I am going to wake up everyday and be disciplined."

"I am going to wake up everyday and pursue my passion and win my inner competitions."

These are our goals. However, we all know this will not be a reality 100% of the time; if it were a reality, life would be easy and greatness would be normal.

Greatness is not normal.

Greatness is earned through constant battles and learning from mistakes. We will all come up short and we will all make mistakes.

I think a huge fear for a lot of people is being considered different or doing something against the grain. **We look around at what is normal and try to fit in instead of stand out.** We are so afraid of making mistakes or coming up short that we often do not push the boundaries to see what we can really achieve. Therein lies the secret to finding out who we really are and how successful we can really be.

YOU HAVE TO PUSH THROUGH THE EVERYONE TO BECOME THE SOMEONE.

The second we realize that our mistakes and shortfalls are golden opportunities to learn and improve is the second we get closer to being our true self. We have to accept our mistakes. This has to do with inner confidence and an inner strength in our beliefs and our true self.

It is very easy to listen to the noise of the outside world and our peers when we make mistakes. We hear negative things about ourselves and believe them. We start to believe that we may be inferior. We start to believe that it is truly our fault. We start to believe all of the negative noise and start to let that influence our inner view of ourself. This is extremely dangerous and a huge lesson to learn.

Weak people will jump at the opportunity to gossip about a negative. They will jump at the opportunity to talk down to you when you make a mistake or come up short. They get in this negative cycle and not only bring down themselves but they bring down the people around them. This is where if you are Self Disciplined, and strong in your inner passion and competitions, you can respectfully listen to the outside noise but use your own inner strength to learn and improve.

It is YOUR CHOICE on how you perceive a mistake that you make.

It is YOUR CHOICE on how it will affect your actions and how you view yourself.

It is YOUR CHOICE whether or not you will use your mistakes as fuel.

I continue to struggle with this concept to this day. I take outside criticism very seriously at times and I dwell on other's words directed at me. I will hold on to something that someone says critically about me for a long period of time. I will analyze and dwell on how I failed and why I didn't do what I should of done. This is the exact thought process that we are trying to avoid. It is not about dwelling on the failure, it is about analyzing and learning from the mistake and moving on and improving.

I have gotten much better at filtering the criticism, finding its true worth and using it to become a better person if there is value in it. If there is no value, I let it pass and turn my focus back within to learn from the mistake itself. That message and lesson is far more valuable than someone else's words. That is the formula to not only start feeling better about yourself but to also improve and get closer to the true you, the best you.

Personal Experience

I want to use another example from my athletic career to shed light on this topic. I want to emphasize again that all of these examples can be substituted out for any examples in your life. As touched on before, one of my biggest mistakes was not being true to myself by pursuing business over an athletic career. That sounds like I did not have a passion for athletics but that is not true at all.

I had an amazing passion for baseball in high school. I was the CIF Player of the Year my Senior year in high school. I had my pick to go pro or pursue college after high school and chose the education and athletic combination. I anticipated having freedom in college to continue doing what made me succeed and I quickly realized that was not the case.

I had unique mechanics as a pitcher. I turned my back to home plate to generate as much velocity as I could. I threw extremely hard for being just over 6 feet tall and 170 lbs. My fastball was reaching 92-95mph and I had a high level of control. Immediately upon starting my college career coaches began to change me to be more conventional. They wanted me to be more robotic and not twist as much as I was. I instantly lost a significant amount of velocity and lost the ability to locate my pitches. My mistake here was not sticking up for myself and what made ME successful.

That example may sound like athletic mumbo jumbo, but when we simplify it, it applies to this entire book. It applies to every concept we have touched on. I had a formula that made me who I was and made me successful. I listened to others, rather than myself, and made changes that ended up serving no one well. Everyone suffered.

This is powerful when you think about it in life terms. **A lot of us know what makes us successful and yet we still change to please others even though it affects our ability to succeed and is against our true self.** This hurts everyone involved. We are no longer the best version of ourself because we let outside noise dictate our actions, thoughts and words. By doing this we suffer and the people around us suffer because we are not unlocking our true potential.

I did not learn from that mistake at that moment which is a negative. However, because of the concepts laid out in this book I am able to look back at that mistake and realize that by not standing up for the true me, and doing what made me successful, I not only hurt myself but I hurt my team and everyone involved.

This is so powerful for my life now. This should be powerful for your life now. We all know what puts us in a better position to succeed. We all know what we are good at. **If we commit to what we are good at with passion and purpose, and not let others drive us away from that, everyone will benefit.** This is a very important point. This isn't about being a rebel or defiant to prove somebody wrong. This is about realizing what you have to offer, who you really are and sticking to that no matter what. **If you commit to you, and to bettering yourself to be the best, you and everyone around you will benefit.**

This is true in any walk of life. We are all employed in some way, shape or form. Even if we are athletes we are an employee of our team just as in the corporate world we are an employee of that team. We are on that team for a reason and that reason is because someone saw something in us that they thought could benefit the team or the company as a whole. We have a talent that can bring tremendous value. However, we want to fit in when we start something new and we will make adjustments over and over to please people instead of doing exactly what we are there to do: be us and help the team or company.

Hopefully this paints the clear picture of what we are trying to see. **You being true to you and doing what makes you successful is the ultimate contribution you can make to yourself AND whatever team you are on in life.** That team can be athletic, corporate, spiritual or family. We are all on a team and we all know how to make our best contribution. You have to realize that you will not be perfect and you have to embrace the process of making adjustments to be the best you for whatever team you are on.

All mistakes and shortfalls are blessings. Start driving that into your head. Start making that a part of your Self Discipline, your Inner Competitions and your Inner Scoreboard. When you come up short or make a mistake start realizing what your response is. Start listening to the chatter around you. A win is using it as fuel and improving yourself because of it. A loss is worrying about what others are saying and how you are viewed in their eyes. Your inner self will grow and get stronger the more you can accept a mistake, learn from it and improve with your next opportunity.

That is the progression in which to view a mistake.

ACCEPT-LEARN-IMPROVE.

Those are the only three words to think about the next time you come up short or make a mistake. It is part of your discipline. It is part of your competition. It is part of your scoreboard. It is another step in becoming the best you.

Chapter 4 Take Away

- **GREATNESS is NOT NORMAL**

- **YOU HAVE TO PUSH THROUGH THE EVERYONE TO BECOME THE SOMEONE**

- **WE have to ACCEPT our MISTAKES**

- **It is YOUR CHOICE on how you VIEW and RESPOND to YOUR MISTAKES**

- **USE your MISTAKES as FUEL**

- **COMMIT to what makes YOU SUCCESSFUL**

- **EMBRACE the PROCESS of MAKING MISTAKES and MAKING ADJUSTMENTS**

- **ACCEPT-LEARN-IMPROVE**

Chapter 5
Everyone Has Struggles

It is important to realize the difference between struggles and mistakes.

Mistake is defined as an error or fault resulting from defective judgment, deficient knowledge, or carelessness. An error or fault, meaning a finite occurrence such as an event or a choice. As we spoke about previously, a mistake is an occurrence that we can now learn from and use as a positive. To me a mistake is acting a certain way and, upon reflection, we realize the action was wrong. After analyzing that mistake we can take the positive lessons and move on. Mistakes become blessings as we spoke about before.

A struggle can be different than a mistake.

Struggle is defined as being strenuously engaged with a problem, task, or undertaking. This is long term. This is something that you battle with over a period of time and it either defeats you or you defeat it.

WE ALL HAVE STRUGGLES.

There are different levels of struggles and their impact levels vary in terms of severity and seriousness. I have yet to meet anyone that does not, on some level, have a struggle.

It is important to be transparent with yourself regarding your struggles. The only way to truly identify your struggle is to be honest with yourself. The next step is identifying if you have a true desire to turn that struggle into a positive journey.

A lot of times we look outward to blame someone, society, circumstance or something else for our struggles. That is a waste of time and a waste of energy, both physically and mentally.

This is where a profound similarity between struggles and mistakes can occur. We have to accept them and we have to make the choice to change them into a positive. We will be on the journey with our struggles regardless; it is our choice whether we will sulk and be negative about them or if we will improve and embrace the struggles.

I want you to think right now about the struggles that you can identify.

What is your number one struggle?

What is your number two struggle?

Is it binge watching a tv show and not tending to important tasks?

Is it procrastinating on deadlines and unnecessarily stressing yourself out?

Is it overeating and being angry when you look at the scale?

These are just a few of literally thousands of struggles that people deal with on a daily basis.

What do all struggles have in common? We all have them. They are all controllable.

As with most concepts in this book it comes down to perspective. Will we view our struggle as an opportunity or will we view it as a hardship, something uncontrollable, or an unfortunate situation that we can not change?

This is another example of average versus elite.

Normal and average is complaining about our struggles. Normal is thinking our struggles are unique and no one else has them. Normal is being self-centered and looking at where we can point the finger to blame something outside of ourselves for our struggles. Just in reading that sentence you should realize how flawed normal is. Looking at where we can point the finger to BLAME SOMETHING OUTSIDE OF **OURSELVES** FOR OUR STRUGGLES.

Let's look at the example questions used above to realize how our struggles can be improved if WE choose to improve them. After that I want to share more examples from my personal experiences, both past and present, to hopefully help you relate to struggles you have faced or are facing.

The first scenario is binge watching a tv show and not tending to important tasks. This is obvious but can be powerful to many of us. We all have a hobby that we give a significant amount of time to. There is absolutely nothing wrong with that. However, when it takes away from significant tasks that need to be tended to, and it happens on a regular basis, it becomes a struggle.

We have all heard of "work before play" or something along those lines to drive in a simple concept; take care of the necessities before you splurge on the luxuries. If you need to do your budget or pay your bills and you put it off to watch a marathon of your favorite show, you are not exercising Self Discipline and you are not being the best you can be.

The second scenario, and a powerful one, is procrastinating on a deadline and causing yourself unnecessary stress. This should scream self control. **Procrastination is the enemy of Self Discipline.** We have all experienced both sides of this scenario. Procrastinating and freaking out about not finishing something on time is one side. Finishing early, under a reasonable time table, and feeling accomplished and relaxed is the other side.

We all have the ability to allocate time and for some reason we choose more often than not to stretch things to the limit. Again, Normal versus Elite. Amateur versus Professional.

Successful people get things done in a different manner than normal people do.

"Go to him or her, they will get it done."

We should want to be the him or her that people come to to get something done. We should want to be the outlier that people look up to for help. We should want to consistently be the Self Disciplined person that people can rely on. It is your choice. Be that person.

The last scenario is overeating and being angry about the results we see on the scale. It is good that this one is last because it touches on a point that we touched on previously, blaming someone or something else for our results. **If our process is flawed and we are not committed to**

anything the way we should be, how can we expect our results to be what we desire?

So many of us eat what we want, do not work out and get angry when we look down at a scale and it says that we are heavier than we want to be. I hate to be blunt but whose fault is that? It is ours. It is the individual whose results aren't what they want them to be.

The best definition of insanity that I have ever heard is doing the same thing over and over again and expecting different results. That one sentence captures what we are talking about perfectly. It is insane to think that we can do everything that normal and average people do and become something special. Insane. That needs to sink in. Yes, everyone has struggles including me and including you. Congratulations you have struggles and I have struggles. We have what everyone has. Now, what are we going to do that everyone doesn't do so that we can become THE SOMEONE?

Before I answer that question I want to reveal more about me. I want to explain my struggles both past and present. I am doing this with the hope that it will create a relationship between you and I. I am not writing an almighty blueprint as if I have it all figured out. I am writing to help me. I am writing to help you. I am writing my experiences because we can all relate to each other. The more we share the more we can use examples to improve and get closer to our best self. My examples are just that, they are my examples that can be interchanged with your examples. We can all help each other improve. Even if it is as simple as realizing you do not agree with someone else's values or views and it makes you stronger in your own being. That is just as powerful as any other lesson.

Personal Experience

I am just like everyone else. I have had struggles and I continue to have struggles. My past struggles were playing a game for years after I had lost the passion for it. I knew, while on the field, that my passion was Off The Field in business and finances of athletics. I also knew that my struggles were Off The Field in the sense that I was using substances to mask my false passions in life. It is extremely difficult to write those words because there are many that will be shocked when they read them but that is what this is all about. It is about accepting past struggles and learning from them to improve my current self.

My two biggest Off The Field struggles were anxiety and alcohol. I will get more into the alcohol battles later but I really want to focus on the anxiety struggle as it continues to be a battle I fight daily.

Anxiety is defined as a state of uneasiness and apprehension, as about future uncertainties.

When I read that definition it perfectly describes my feeling while playing the beautiful sport of baseball. I was uneasy and apprehensive about pursuing a career that I was not passionate about. The future was uncertain because I did not control the outcome of my career. This was a constant struggle for me until the day I retired from my athletic career. I struggled back and forth between identifying myself as a professional athlete and as identifying myself as the complete opposite.

Hopefully this hits home with you as the reader. If you have felt anxiety maybe you can identify where it is stemming from. A lot of anxiety comes from "people pleasing" and from trying to do what everyone thinks we should do. That is where a lot of struggle comes from. **We struggle to please everyone while also being true to ourselves.** I know this is where one of my biggest struggles stemmed from. I wanted to please my family and my peers but I knew pursuing professional baseball was not what I was passionate about.

This is another opportunity to view a negative as a positive. Anxiety has such a negative connotation in our society and we shy away or are scared of having it. Anxiety can actually be an indication of us being untrue to ourselves and be an opportunity to learn from unnecessary struggles that we are having.

When I analyze and observe my past and current anxieties I realize that most of them stem from me doubting my inner self and concerning myself with the outside views and opinions. At first, my anxiety scared me and I felt as if it was something I could not control or something that I was the victim of. As I started to live with it, and have more experiences with it, I realized it is like everything else, it is an opportunity. I will say that it is still one of the least pleasant opportunities that I face but yet it is still an opportunity. I have to view it as something that I am blessed with. It is something that I have to deal with on a daily basis and it is something that is here for me to learn from and improve upon.

This is the lesson from all struggles. Everyone has them. Everyone has an opportunity to view struggles as a normal person or as an elite and disciplined person.

Are the struggles the product of someone or something else, or are they something to learn from and make adjustments so you and everyone around you can benefit?

Your struggles do not define you. Your perception of them can, however, and this can be negative or positive. Make it a positive and, just like mistakes, use struggles as fuel and opportunities. You are not alone in your struggles. Do not feel like a victim. Feel fortunate that this is part of your identity and you have the opportunity to improve your struggles. **YOU again have the CHOICE to determine the outcome of YOUR circumstances.**

Chapter 5 Take Away

- **WE ALL have STRUGGLES**

- **BE TRANSPARENT; EMBRACE your STRUGGLES**

- **Turn your STRUGGLES into a POSITIVE JOURNEY**

- **BE the OUTLIER - BE "THAT PERSON"**

- **CHANGE your PROCESS, CHANGE your RESULTS**

- **SHARE your STRUGGLES**

- **HELP OTHERS - HELP YOURSELF**

- **YOUR STRUGGLES DO NOT DEFINE YOU**

Off The Field: Carving Your Own Path To Find Your Best Self

Chapter 6
*Alcohol, Addiction and Obsession
(Not all bad)*

We have addressed some very important concepts that are key to improvement and success. We have laid a foundation of fundamental steps we can implement to make positive changes in our lives. I now want to take a closer look at struggles, mistakes and hardships. We have addressed these concepts but will now look deeper into their roles in our lives.

I feel the secret to lasting and consistent success in life is your reaction and approach to struggles and mistakes. **If you truly use mistakes and struggles as fuel, find the positive in them, and**

look for the lesson in every one, your life will improve dramatically.

I want to dive more into my personal struggles and how I interpret them, battle them and try to use them as a positive on a daily basis. This chapter will be the hardest to write. This chapter may be the hardest to read. I am hoping it exposes me and helps me relate as a human being to you. I hope it helps you expose yourself and identify your vice and/or Achilles heal and attack it head on.

Personal Experience

I have had a consistent enemy appear in my life. I have had one major opponent defeat me more times than I have defeated it. In fact, for me, it can not be defeated. The truth is I can not even compete against it. I can not try to control it. It will inevitably beat me every single time. This enemy, this opponent and this Achilles heel for me is alcohol.

I have been dealt an extremely poor hand genetically to handle alcohol. I have an obsessive gene, addictive gene and a family history of alcoholism. I have what you would call a perfect storm for alcohol to destroy a life. This is extremely unfortunate because alcohol is everywhere these days. It is what people use to relax, it is what people use to fit in and it is more prevalent today than it has ever been.

During my playing career alcohol was my best friend. I used it and abused it to get away from any of the problems I was facing. When I drank I could escape the lie of pursuing a career that wasn't my true love. I could escape all of the outside expectations that were being placed on me. I could escape waking up every day and pursuing something that I was not 100% invested in. What I did not realize at the time was that I was not escaping anything. I was covering up the issues and actually making them worse.

When you bury a problem or a negative thought it does not go away. All it does is grow stronger and stronger until eventually it pops and you have no choice but to face it.

For me, the popping was after the arm surgery and facing the lie head on. It was facing the fact that I needed to make a choice for me and pursue what it was that I truly felt was my purpose.

The problem is that the alcohol abuse did not go away simply by beginning to pursue my passion. Like I said, I was dealt a poor hand in terms of genetics and circumstances when it comes to a substance like alcohol. I was addicted and continued to abuse my vice, my escape.

*From the outside world many would probably view me as an alcoholic who just drank and couldn't control it. They would view me as irresponsible and someone that didn't care about the consequences of my consumption of alcohol. To some extent these views may be true. I was being irresponsible but in a way I did not know any better. It was my escape and one of the only times I felt comfortable in my skin is when I was consuming alcohol and escaping my reality. It was this battle with alcohol that brought to life the phrase **OFF THE FIELD** for me.*

*I was grinding and working so hard to achieve on the field success for everyone besides myself. As a result, I developed a huge struggle **Off the Field in the abuse of alcohol.** With this struggle came many mistakes, shortfalls and let downs that helped start to form a reflection that would show* *me my true passion also lies **OFF THE FIELD.** This is why this simple phrase and title is so significant to me. **Off the Field** is where my struggle was that needed to be dealt with. **Off the Field** is where my passion was for business and finances. **Off the Field** is where we all end up and we all fight to improve as human beings.*

My father helped me reflect on a significant point about an athletic career ending. At some point every single athlete's career comes to an end. That is significant in itself.

If you define and judge yourself by the on field results what happens when your on the field career ends?

What do you have left?

Who is the real you?

This is so important because it shows why it does not matter if you are an athlete or non-athlete. **You are defined by who you are in life as a whole. That is what you should judge yourself on.**

How disciplined are you?

Are you trying to improve?

Are you analyzing yourself and identifying your hardships, addictions, problems and mistakes and trying to change them for the better?

Every single one of us is going to have a vice or an addiction of some sort. Not all of these are bad but if we do not control them they may end up controlling us or creating negative circumstances or consequences. Again, the word **honesty** is going to come up.

Self-Honesty is the most important type of honesty.

We all hear the voice in our head and we know what is right and wrong for ourselves. The more right decisions we make, the more we will show Self Discipline and win our Inner Competitions. It is a switch that we flip to hold ourselves accountable and accept that we are flawed and that we want to improve. Once we flip that switch it becomes easier to accept everything that we have ever done.

Why? Let's address why.

The second you commit to improving every chance you get, you will realize that everything you have done is a lesson. You can accept everything you have done, the good and the bad, because you can view them for what they are worth. I struggled, and still need to keep my guard up with alcohol, but it is a positive lesson. I identified my vice and my fake magic elixir. It was a curse and a cover-up and did me no positive. The second I realized that is the second I could start to battle it, show Self Discipline and try to win my Inner Competitions against it.

That process gets me closer to the best version of myself.

What is your vice?

Are you using something to escape?

It can be food, tv, a substance or anything else used to distract you from your pain or your ultimate goal. Identify it and use it to your advantage. When you begin working on it, and begin making positive adjustments, you will feel ultimate fulfillment and it will influence other decisions and habits in your life positively.

There is a word that has a negative connotation for the most point in our society.
That word is **Obsession.**

It is funny because I almost cringe even writing the word because of the way people view it. In reality, obsession can be one of the most positive words if we look at it the right way.

If you want to accomplish something and you kind of give it your attention but are still focused on a million other things how do you like your chances?

I do not like them very much.

If you have a goal and are obsessed with achieving it in a healthy way I like your chances way better.

What if we get obsessed with being the best version of ourselves?

What if we get obsessed with being Self Disciplined?

What if we get obsessed with analyzing ourselves and viewing any negatives as positives that have worth and can teach us something?

These questions literally excite me as I write them. As the reader it should help you see the foundation we are trying to achieve.

If we can achieve a healthy obsession with the things we are trying to accomplish we will have a much better chance to succeed. Committing to anything halfway is not good enough and will not yield high success rates.

Normal and average people commit halfway and achieve half results.
That is not what we want.
We want to be ELITE.

We want to be our best. If we get obsessed with becoming better on a daily basis, we will give ourselves the best chance to succeed.

We all have an off the field.

Are you a housewife, a gardener, a plumber, a consultant, an artist, an actor, an athlete or any other walk of life? Guess what? The answer is yes. We are all someone.

You are someone and you have the ability to improve and view any negative in a different way than you ever have before. Eliminate the outside noise. Focus within yourself to find out the true worth of your experiences. You have gone through your experiences for a reason and I would bet that you could find a positive in most all of them.

Accept your vice, and if it negatively controls you, eliminate it and accept that it was part of your life and taught you something positive. You are in control and it is time to focus on the present moment and the future.

Be obsessed with being a better version of you and improving a little bit everyday.

Chapter 6 Take Away

- **MISTAKES are FUEL**

- **ATTACK Struggle Head On**

- **Identify your Vice/Achilles Heel and COMPETE Against It**

- **COMPETE Against YOURSELF**

- **Use POSITIVE OBSESSION to IMPROVE YOURSELF**

- **BE ELITE**

Chapter 7
Focus Forward

Everything in our past can teach us some sort of lesson. Each occurrence in our life can teach us something positive or have a positive undertone. The only way this can be 100% true is if we make the commitment to not dwell on the past. This does not mean disregarding the past entirely but putting more focus on the present and the future.

The past is to learn from and improve upon but the present and future are the only places we can choose to be our best self and improve upon our current status. I like to call it Focusing Forward. If we Focus Forward we can be a product of everything that has happened to us and put forth our best self. The more we focus on our next step, the more we will benefit and move toward our ultimate goal of improving.

Again, I want to stress that it is not about disregarding the past.

As stated in a previous chapter: **insanity is doing the same thing over and over and expecting different results.**

We have to learn from our decisions that we make and the outcomes of those decisions. **If we do not learn from our decisions and make adjustments we will get caught in a repetitive cycle and hover around mediocrity our entire life.** Mistakes are not finite negatives as we have already touched on numerous times. The failure to learn from them and implement improvements is where a detrimental pattern can be formed.

We must use all of our experiences. Analyze them. Learn from them. Process the positives and negatives and believe that there is a lesson in every single one of them.

Focus Forward on Improving.

That is what this is all about. Improving.

You can not fully improve if you are constantly looking in the rearview mirror of your life and dwelling on past events.

This goes for both positives and negatives.

A lot of times we think of dwelling on the past as only negative but you can hold on to past successes for too long as well.

Yesterday was yesterday.

If you keep patting yourself on the back for something that you have done, complacency will strike and your improvement meter will be stagnant.

Stagnancy and complacency are poisonous words for your life if you truly want to be the best you.

Focus on giving 100% each moment of each day.

Learn from the past and Focus Forward on each moment that is to come.

Personal Experience

As I've written these concepts down I continue to keep looking back as to where I've struggled in the past. It is a natural instinct to look at your personal experiences and to judge yourself. I have been told, and I am fully aware, that I have a constant struggle with being far too critical of myself. I hold onto things for an extended period of time and if things do not go perfectly I blame myself.

I am a perfectionist and I have a hard time not looking at my past mistakes and dwelling on them. It is almost as if I feel everyone can see a reel of every negative decision or action I have ever had in my life and they are judging me by it on a daily basis. Just writing those words I can see how absurd those thoughts are, but it is amazing some of the thoughts we can have and how they can affect our perception of ourself.

Hopefully your thought processes are not this extreme but if they are, or you have something similar you are struggling with, Focusing Forward can be a powerful and profound technique to improve self-worth and self-perception.

Imagine a process where we start to focus on one moment at a time going forward in our life. If we are already the sum of all of our past experiences we do not need to look back and dwell on them. We have self-consciously processed the positives and negatives and we know right from wrong and what will benefit us going forward. If we start focusing on one moment at a time, and we start making disciplined decisions and succeeding, our self-worth and self-perception are bound to improve. They have to because once we start laying the positive foundation, and do it for an extended period of time, when we look back, we will see a positive picture.

That is a long and drawn out explanation that could be murky. **What we are trying to achieve is a pattern of positive decisions.** If we achieve this, we will build a foundation of positive. As we do this consistently, and over time, we will start to look back and see ourselves in a positive manner. As we pattern our lives in a disciplined way we will stock up on positive memories of our actions and our self-worth and self-perception improves.

Life is all about perspective, adjustments and improvement.

As we read these words right now I want us all to accept everything we have ever done.

Take a moment, take a deep breath and if you want to say out loud, **"I accept every decision I have ever made and I accept who I am right now."**

If you do not want to say it out loud just think it to yourself. Either way you have to truly believe it and accept it.

Why? Because you are who you are.
You are where you are.
You can only get to where you want to go by giving your life everything you have starting right now.

It is your choice to Focus Forward.
I have to do this as well. I struggle with this daily.

Personal Experience
I have to accept everything I have ever done and commit to me now.

That is the kind of declaration it takes to begin a journey towards something different. I have so many past memories that, if I let them, could haunt me and cause complacency and average behavior. I hurt so many people close to me with my alcohol abuse. I lost countless friendships because of decisions I made in the past. I did not commit to me and stand up for what I truly believed in during my on the field career. I did not stand up for myself for years while I continued to play and not pursue my Off the Field passions. I let my unhappiness with my on the field career cause me to hide the Off the Field struggles from anyone who was close to me. I let those Off the Field struggles get worse and cause pain and turmoil in multiple facets of my life. I have had actions, words, struggles and pain that I am not proud of and that I can not change.

I accept that.

I am who I am and I can get better every single moment if I commit to being my best.
That was not planned. I did not plan on writing those words at this moment but I am glad that it is what came out as I typed. That is my declaration and it is an example of what has to be done. Your

life is different than everyone else's. You are unique and your declaration will be different. If you can look at yourself and be honest (there is self honesty again) you can look back at everything, accept it and move on. I love the saying **you are the sum of everything that you have done.** It is the truth and you have to accept you for you.

I understand that everyone is dealt a different hand in life. Everyone is not given equal opportunity and some are more fortunate than others. Sometimes life deals you things out of your control and it can feel helpless. It becomes easy to point the finger and feel like a victim. This thought process, and it is going to be hard to hear and hard to believe, is also a choice. Yes, some people are lucky. Some people are unlucky. However, it still comes down to acceptance and improvement.

Everyone can sulk, blame, quit and be average. That is why it is called average because most fall victim to it.

If you want to push through the everyone to become the someone you have to be different and you have to embrace the difficult.

It is about YOU, and YOU are who YOU are right now. Nothing can change that fact. **Accept you. Embrace you. FOCUS FORWARD.**

Chapter 7 Take Away

- **USE the PAST. DO NOT DWELL on it**

- **FOCUS FORWARD on each step**

- **IMPROVE CONSTANTLY**

- **Learn the LESSONS from your EXPERIENCES and then FOCUS FORWARD**

- **YESTERDAY was YESTERDAY**

- **Give 100% EACH MOMENT of EACH DAY**

- **YOU are UNIQUE. EMBRACE being DIFFERENT**

- **Develop a PATTERN of POSITIVE DECISIONS**

- **FOCUS FORWARD**

Chapter 8
Daily Battles

We are all going to be tested in life. No one can escape that fact.

The concepts laid out in this book will make a significant impact on your life if implemented correctly. The concepts are the PHILOSOPHY or the WHY behind what we are doing and trying to accomplish. The action is putting the concepts in motion in your life and monitoring your progress. **The concepts are simple. The action is not.**

Implementing Self Discipline, holding yourself accountable and embracing mistakes are all extremely difficult to pull off on a consistent basis. That is why we have the Inner Scoreboard and Inner Competition to show us how well we are doing. Our success barometer can be summarized in one simple statement:

BE DIFFERENT and BE A BETTER YOU.

Concepts like these are more difficult to accomplish than people think.

Why?

The concepts are easy to understand. They show us the end result that we want.

The problems arise when it comes down to execution. We struggle to implement the step by step process that it takes to see our desired end result. We want a quick fix and eventually we regress to the mean and go back to what is comfortable: Being Average.

Discipline, Competition, Commitment, accepting ourselves and accepting mistakes are all tasks that sound achievable. They ARE ACHIEVABLE. However, **if you do not have a daily plan it will be easy to fall back into your normal routine or your comfort zone.**

You have to battle on a daily basis to achieve all of these concepts.

You have to remind yourself constantly of what you want to accomplish.

This will lay the foundation and set you up to achieve long term success.

Personal Experience

This concept was introduced to me by Alan Jaeger of Jaeger Sports. Jaeger Sports is the company where I am currently the Vice President and Lead Instructor. I attended a clinic when I was 12 years old, fell in love with the program and never left. Jaeger Sports is known for Arm Care and Arm Conditioning but Alan is also known as one of the world's leaders in Mental Training.

I fell in love with the physical part of the program at a young age, but as I grew older, I quickly became infatuated with Alan's Mental Training program. The mental training concepts taught to me by Alan through Jaeger Sports were actually a determining factor in choosing my college major of Psychology at Cal State University Northridge. I wanted to learn everything I could about the thought processes of people and apply them to sports and life.

Alan teaches about the power of the breath, being present, being process oriented and many other powerful concepts. The most powerful concept that has hit me harder and harder over time is the necessity for a daily plan. He stresses the importance in having a daily reminder of what you want to achieve with mental training. He also stresses the importance of having a daily practice plan.

This is the key to achieving your desired results. You need to have a constant reminder of the desired end goal. The more something is at the forefront of your mind the more it will become familiar to you. **The more being your best you is at the forefront of your mind the more familiar you become with that version of yourself.** *You will create the habit of improving which is scary to think about in a great way.*

In Alan's words, **"YOU BECOME WHAT YOU PRACTICE."**

Just like Alan preaches this for mental training we want to preach this with what we are trying to accomplish. Self discipline, Commitment from Within, Inner Competition, Accepting Mistakes,

Focusing Forward are all concepts we want to be aware of on a daily basis.
I call it **Daily Battles.**

Every day is an opportunity to battle your average self and win.

If you wake up everyday embracing that challenge, and being aware that what you are trying to accomplish isn't easy, you will give yourself a much better chance to succeed.

This goes back to the point at the beginning of the chapter where we referred to why people do not achieve their end result. They want a quick fix, they look at the big picture as a whole and they do not see the step by step approach that they need to. This is where the Daily Battles approach can be massive. With Daily Battles you see consistent improvement and eventually get to where you are trying to get to.

There is not an end date. There is no ultimate result to where we can ever say we are done. **We are always going to have the opportunity to improve.** We will have that opportunity every day until we are no longer on this earth. However, there is success. **Success comes in the form of consistently making positive, disciplined decisions over enough time to continue to get closer to the best version of yourself.**

So what do these Daily Battles look like?

How can we create them and identify them for ourselves?

We can look at Daily Battles in two different ways. We can look at Daily Battles as a broad approach where each day is an individual battle. We can also look at Daily Battles where different events throughout each day are little battles.

All of these battles are opportunities to make a positive or negative decision.

All of these battles are opportunities to get closer or farther from our goal.

Ultimately these battles are opportunities to teach us something.

The more positive battles that we can put in the bank the more we will start to build a positive foundation. As we do this, making the right decisions or adjustments will become common for us.

Let's look even deeper into what Daily Battles look like and how we can keep score accurately. Here's an example for me currently. First, let's look at the more broad approach or a day as a whole and also how that blends in with the individual daily battles.

Today is Sunday. It is during the NFL season so there is football on for about 10 hours straight. I have been known to sit for all 10 or 11 of these hours in one spot, eat poorly and get nothing done. Last night before I went to bed I noted everything I wanted to get done today. Clean my entire house, the bathroom, bedroom, living room and kitchen. Organize some of my belongings and get rid of them. Finally, walk my dog. As a whole at the end of the day I can look at how many positives there were versus the negatives and judge myself accordingly. If there were more positives than negatives then I can judge that Daily Battle for this day as a win.

This is an important example because most of my individual Daily Battles for today were planned by me the night before. It is much easier to prepare for these daily battles and be ready to accomplish them by allocating the appropriate time to get the jobs done. I am not saying that is bad and when you can plan ahead it is obviously ideal to do so.

We all know real life is anything but scripted and things come up at all times without us being able to control them. This is what makes people uncomfortable. Things come up, out of our control, and causes us to act negatively or do what everyone else does. We do this because it is easy or it is comfortable.

We have to be ok with things being hard and things being uncomfortable. We have to be ok with things being outside of our control. We have to embrace being outside of our comfort zone.

This is how we will achieve success in the individual Daily Battles. If we are waking up embracing each day as an opportunity, or as a battle, we will be much more equipped to handle these battles because we will already be in that mindset. It will get to a point to where we almost expect the unexpected and crave a situation to come up so we can make the disciplined and positive decision. At the end of the day, when we look back at all of the examples of us making the right choice, we will feel accomplished and will like the results on our Inner Scoreboard.

Daily Battles. Step by step. One building block at a time. Sounds boring huh?

Sounds like the opposite of the fad diets out there or the instant result campaigns.

That is because the concepts we are talking about have real substance and produce real results. **Accept the fact that anything worth having in life involves hard work and dedication.** If you want to achieve anything, it starts within, and it starts with a purpose.

Put your plan in motion and EMBRACE THE BATTLE.

Chapter 8 Take Away

- **IDEAS mean NOTHING without ACTION**

- **Be DIFFERENT - BE a BETTER YOU**

- **Have a DAILY PRACTICE PLAN**

- **Get Familiar with YOUR BEST SELF**

- **EVERY Day is an OPPORTUNITY to BATTLE Your AVERAGE Self and WIN**

- **Make a list of what you want to ACCOMPLISH EVERY DAY**

- **Plan for what you can Plan For; EMBRACE WHAT YOU CAN NOT**

- **Be OK with things being UNCOMFORTABLE and DIFFICULT**

- **CREATE the HABIT of IMPROVING**

- **EMBRACE ACTION - EMBRACE THE BATTLE**

Chapter 9
Simplifying Goals

Being the best you is the ultimate goal.
Being the best you is not easy to achieve.
In order to achieve our ultimate goal we must
simplify and implement a step by step approach.

The best way to set ourselves up to succeed is to
clearly define our goals. We all have heard about
having a plan or having goals. In fact, it is a huge
conversation piece whether you are interviewing
for a job or meeting someone for the first time.

"What is your five year plan?"

"Where do you see yourself in ten years?"

These are common questions. These are questions that are asking you about your five or ten year goal. Five or ten year goals are massive outcomes to think about and can be overwhelming.

It is ludicrous to think solely about a desired outcome without thinking about the steps that it takes to accomplish that outcome. It is not conducive for success and we need to simplify.

Let's look at all of the concepts we have talked about and how simple goals can help us get to where we want to be.

The first concept we talked about was **Self Discipline.** The first step to take is to determine what Self Discipline looks like for you. In doing this, you can visualize what simple goals can help you achieve Self Discipline in your own life. You may have a daily checklist of a few things you need to do to ensure you are meeting your Self Discipline goals.

For me, my first checkpoint would be not drinking alcohol. I know that is my biggest issue and the biggest way that I can show Self Discipline. It is a simple goal in the sense that succeeding is not a drop of alcohol and failure is drinking any alcohol. It is a simple goal to keep track of and easy to see tangible results. After that, simple things like eating well, brushing my teeth before bed, etc. are other simple goals that I can achieve and help me improve as a person.

Notice that these goals are all easy to see success or failure. This is essential so that we can see where we need to improve or where we are doing well. Do this for yourself so you can hold yourself accountable. Define goals so that you clearly know what failure is, and more importantly, what success is.

The next concept we talked about was **Commitment From Within.** This concept is tougher to see a tangible result but again it comes back to being honest with yourself. The simple goal would be waking up committed to whatever you are doing on that day. We all know if we are committing to something or not. We all know if we are giving something our all or not.

This point is interesting because it seems like Commitment From Within is a complex concept and judging ourselves on that may be difficult. In reality, it is much more simple. We are either committing or we are not. We feel it in our gut and in our heart. If we are honest with ourselves we know if we are achieving this simple goal.

Inner Competition and Inner Scoreboard should be easy concepts to implement our simplifying goals. Each competition on a daily basis is a simple goal that we are trying to achieve. Each of those competitions we can easily tell if we we can mark it as a win or as a loss. The win or the loss is then marked on our Inner Scoreboard. If we are being conscious of the competitions and keeping track of our wins and losses then we are achieving our goal of keeping an Inner Scoreboard. If we have a simple goal to win our next competition, and track the results on our Inner Scoreboard, we are achieving what we want to do with this concept. Just by being aware that the competition comes from within we are implementing a simple goal and giving ourselves a high success rate. **It is all about being aware and feeding off of each competition and each success.**

Perhaps the simplest goal of all of these concepts is **Accepting Mistakes, Shortfalls and**

Struggles. The goal is simple, the implementation is not. The goal: accept them. That is as simple as it can be. You either accept them or dwell on them. If you dwell on mistakes, shortfalls and struggles you continue to let them influence your behaviors and self perception which in turn is failing your goal. The simple goal for these concepts can tie in beautifully with the concept of **Focusing Forward.**

A simple goal for these concepts could be to have a daily routine where you have an inner conversation about **you are who you are.** Stating a daily declaration can be a simple goal for yourself. Perhaps in the morning or before bed you can remind yourself to accept everything you have done.

You can accept that you are the sum of everything that has happened in your life and the choices you have made. You can accept you for you every single day of your life. You accept the Struggles, Mistakes and Shortfalls and Focus Forward on what you can control.

All of these are only recommendations and are things that help me in my life on a daily basis. However, you are you and that is what this is all about. **You have to find out what it is that works best for you.**

What daily routines, reminders and simple goals help you be who you want to be?

That is what truly matters for you to give yourself the best chance to succeed. Break it down for yourself and lay out a plan that you think will work for you. As you start to implement your plan do not get discouraged if it does not go perfectly. That is where you separate yourself from the crowd. The more you can embrace the adversity and make adjustments and improvements where you need to, the more you will start to see a quality of life that you did not think was possible. The more you start to look within yourself for what makes you tick and the more you start to set simple goals, the more you will start to feel true purpose.

That is where we are trying to get to with all of these simple goals. That is where we are trying to get with implementing these concepts.

For me it is about me. For you it is about you.

It is about taking your focus off of the outside world and expectations and pursuing your passion and finding your purpose.

The more you start to pursue your passion and commit to living a unique and positive life, the more you and everyone around you will feel the benefits. That is a powerful vision and it could start a positive cycle of you inspiring people to improve themselves. It starts with setting simple goals and taking the first step.

Stay Committed - Adjust - Improve - Be YOU

Chapter 9 Take Away

- **SIMPLIFY and PLAN**

- **GOALS mean NOTHING without a PLAN**

- **CELEBRATE each step of the JOURNEY**

- **Make a DAILY CHECKLIST**

- **Have goals with TANGIBLE RESULTS**

- **COMMIT EVERY DAY**

- **Be AWARE and FEED OFF of SUCCESS**

- **YOU ARE WHO YOU ARE**

- **What works BEST for YOU?**

- **STAY COMMITTED - ADJUST - IMPROVE - BE YOU**

Chapter 10
You Get Out of Life What You Put Into It

All of the concepts have been laid out. There is a clear vision of what these concepts look like. You should now be able to visualize what these concepts look like in your life. **Life comes down to you being honest with yourself on a daily basis and pushing towards your ultimate goals.**

The ultimate goal in this book has been becoming the best version of yourself. However all of the concepts in this book can be applied to any goal that you are trying to accomplish. The bottom line is:

YOU ARE GOING TO GET OUT OF LIFE WHAT YOU PUT INTO IT.

Personal Experience

This line has become a staple in my life over the last couple of years. I began saying it on occasion and as time passed it became a larger part of my vocabulary. The line really started to have an affect on me when I saw the reaction of the people I said it to. The reaction was so powerful and so positive that I really started to analyze the saying and what it meant. The more I analyzed it, the more I felt its power.

I started to use the saying to analyze countless situations in my life. Situations that I succeeded in and situations that I did not. In an overwhelming majority, if not all of the situations in which I succeeded, I had done everything I could do to prepare for that situation. On the flip side, in the situations in which I did not succeed, I could think of an example of something I could have done more to prepare for that situation.

This is powerful. I realized that when I had put in the effort, exhausted all options and was committed to something, I succeeded more often than not. It was an epiphany and something I wanted to share as much as I could share.

As part of my job I travel around the country and put on Long Toss Demonstrations with Jaeger Sports. At the end of the demonstration I get a few minutes to share whatever I want with the athletes before the clinic comes to an end. At first I was very timid to speak and would keep it as short as possible to save me from the uneasiness of public speaking. As I started to dive more into this concept of getting out of life what you put into it, my speeches started to get longer. I started to care less about the uneasiness of public speaking and started to care more about making sure everyone heard the message loud and clear.

YOU ARE GOING TO GET OUT OF LIFE WHAT YOU PUT INTO IT.

If you put in normal work and average training, do not expect anything other than average results.

An example I started to use for the athletes that I speak to is school work. It is a relevant example to use for these athletes because most of them are in college or high school. It strikes a nerve with them and they can relate to it. I explain that you can look at life as a big term paper or a big test. A good grade on the term paper or the big test is the end result. We have time to prepare for the big term paper or the big test. It is on us to allocate our time accordingly to ensure we prepare ourselves correctly.

There is always a friend who wants to go out instead of study or watch a movie instead of read up on the material. You have a choice. You can let their influence take you away from your goal or you can focus and do what you need to do. There are days when you are tired. There are days you when you don't want to take the practice test. There are days when you don't want to start the introduction for your paper. You have a choice to fight through the tired feeling and do what you need to do.

At the end of this process of making the correct or incorrect decisions you get to put forth your product to be judged. **If you did what you needed to do, and remained disciplined, more often than not you get your desired result.** In the case of school work the result is a good grade.

The looks I received the first time I shared this example showed me that these words and this concept struck a chord with these athletes. I know this can strike a chord with many people.

There are outside influences that will try to take you away from your end result. It is up to you to not pay attention to those influences. If possible you should eliminate them from your life entirely. These influences are often people but that is not always the case. It can be a substance. It can be television. Anything that takes your eye off of the prize is a negative influence. Anything that causes you to not work as hard as you can is a negative influence. Address these negative influences. Eliminate them.

Think about the example of the term paper or big test as your life. Our life is the big test or the term paper. The more we remain disciplined, the more we put into making our life better and more positive, the more we will like the results. It really comes down to this simple concept. **YOU GET OUT OF LIFE WHAT YOU PUT INTO IT.**

This is an easy barometer to monitor yourself on a consistent basis. The key is to be honest with yourself.

Are you putting into life as much as you can to ensure your desired result?

More often than not the answer is going to be no. The more you put in the more you are going to get out. It is never about being perfect. It is about doing the best that you can and giving it as much effort as possible on a consistent basis. If you do not do this your results will not be what you want. **If you consistently give your best effort, and put in the work, you will often achieve your desired results.**

The concepts laid out in this book all tie together. The key is committing to the concepts and embracing the process. There will be trial and error as there is with anything in life. Find out what works for you and own it. Make it yours.

If you are not seeing the results that you seek, figure out where to make adjustments and give 100%.

YOUR RESULTS IN LIFE ARE A DIRECT REFLECTION OF THE EFFORT YOU ARE GIVING.

The results are a direct reflection of your commitment to what you are doing. The results are a direct reflection on whether or not you are pursuing your passion. After all, it is hard to put a lot of effort into something that you are not passionate about.

Chapter 10 Take Away

- **PREPARE**

- **FIGHT through the AVERAGE**

- **ELIMINATE NEGATIVE INFLUENCES**

- **YOUR RESULTS in Life are a DIRECT REFLECTION of the EFFORT that YOU are Giving**

- **Be CONSISTENT**

- **Find What Works Best for YOU and OWN IT**

- **YOU GET OUT OF LIFE WHAT YOU PUT INTO IT**

Chapter 11

Pursue Your Passion

There is a saying that means more to me than any other on this planet. It is on the mirror in my bathroom. It is on the back of my business card. It is on my mind every single day that is successful in my life. It is a saying that I hope you will take seriously and put into action in your own life. That saying: **"PURSUE YOUR PASSION"**

The concepts in this book have led to this. **The probability of success increases greatly if you are waking up on a daily basis and Pursuing Your Passion.** The concepts we have covered are much easier to implement if you are implementing them towards your passion.

Personal Experience

We have touched on my battle with passion for baseball. I do not want anyone to read this book and think that I do not have a true love for the sport. I do. I still do. I was changed over and over as my career progressed and the passion was eliminated shortly after high school. After high school, I continued to pursue the career for the wrong reasons.

There is a story that stands out to me that is a great example of me feeling passion for playing the game of baseball. This story is known in my family as "The 7th Inning."

My senior year at Vasquez High School was full of buzz and attention the school had never received before. Before our team at Vasquez High School there was not even an on-campus field. Our team's parents, led by John Sisco, got together and made a field. It was a scene straight out of Field of Dreams.

During my final year at VHS there were numerous professional scouts pointing radar guns at my pitches from behind the backstop at every game. Our baseball team was the focus of tv shows,

*news reports and countless newspaper articles.
The reporters and scouts would always grumble
about having to drive out into the middle of
nowhere in Acton, CA to watch me play. As the
season progressed there was one game that was
more anticipated than any other. It was a home
game against the defending champions in our
division.*

*One individual I have not introduced you to is my
high school baseball coach, Bob James. Coach
Bob had played in the big leagues, was a
dominant closer and was an absolute joy to play
for. He always supported us as players, students
and as young men.*

I remember his support vividly.

*Bob had informed me that Cal State Fullerton
coaches would be in attendance to watch me play
in this highly anticipated game against the
defending champions. This was exciting for me
and everyone involved in the program because
Cal State Fullerton was the defending College
World Series Champion and our program did not
usually get that kind of attention.*

The game was highly anticipated, highly attended and the product on the field did not let anyone down.

In the 7th inning, which is the final inning in high school baseball, we had a 1-0 lead. Bob sent me back out for the 7th inning to finish the game off and the inning could not have been more eventful.

The inning started with a late swing that resulted in a double down the right field line. The next hitter laid down a perfect sacrifice bunt that resulted in him being safe and runners being on first and third. The next batter was the defending CIF Player of the Year. It was the matchup everyone wanted to see.

Would my emotions get the best of me?

Which would win -- Pitching or Defense?

All of these types of questions were going through everyone's minds.
Well, everyone's except for mine.

I was very aware of the situation at that point of the game. I knew I had a good chance to get the hitter out but I knew I had a greater chance to get the next three hitters out after him.

*What happened next shocked everyone.
I pointed to the umpire and to first base.*

This was the sign to intentionally walk someone in High School at that time. You did not have to throw the pitches. The umpire was caught off guard so I made the gesture again. He looked into our dugout at Coach Bob and Coach Bob gave him a nod and the umpire sent the runner to first loading the bases. It was a cardinal sin to put the go ahead run on second base with no outs but I knew I had the best opportunity to give us a win facing the next three hitters.

I looked over at Coach Bob and we shared a moment that sticks with me to this day. It was a look of confidence and respect between each other where we almost knew what was going to happen next. It was my game to win or lose for our team.

The next batter stepped in and I struck him out.

The next batter stepped in and I struck him out.

The next batter stepped in with two outs, the bases loaded in a 1-0 game and I struck him out. I remember screaming in excitement and feeling such a passion for the game and for competition.

As I walked Off the Field I remember a hug from Coach Bob. I felt support. I felt comfort. I never really felt that again in the game. He allowed me to be me because he knew that was best for the team. **Nothing was broken so why would he try to fix it?**

Cal State Fullerton offered me a scholarship in the moments after the game. It was a cool feeling but not what that moment was about. It was about Coach Bob, Vasquez High School and our team. We all had a respect for each other on that team and more importantly Bob instilled in us that we had a purpose together as a unit.

We all want to feel like we have a purpose in life. I promise you that you will begin to feel purpose the day you start to Pursue Your Passion. If you are not truly pursuing your passion there will be a void or an underlying emptiness in you. It will eat at you until you make the adjustment. You may not even be able to identify it unless you give yourself the opportunity to analyze your life. You may go on for years just going through the motions.

That is the scariest thing in life and my biggest fear. I do not want to wake up one day and look back and say, "Wow, how did I get here?" "Where has the time gone?" "This was supposed to be a temporary phase and it has been 10 years."

I want to make sure there is clarity with this concept. I am not saying that if you do not love your job you should quit. I am not saying you should make life overhauls that could have huge negative consequences. I am saying that if you are in a position to pursue a change that is more in line with your passions, you should take it. It doesn't have to be a huge life change. It could be pursuing a hobby that you used to be passionate about. It could be starting a side project that gives you that fire you used to have. Just analyze your life and your passion meter and figure out how you can make it better for you.

This can help your relationship as well. A lot of times life gets so intense that we get into a routine and the passion and intimacy of our relationship suffers. Try to remember what made you so passionate. Remember the things you used to do together that you enjoyed and make the commitment to do those things together again. Even if it is something as simple as once a month going to a former date spot. These simple adjustments can hugely alter the passion level for you.

This is just one example of an adjustment that can be made. We could go on and on about other examples. **It comes down to you. You know what your true passions are. You know if you are committed to pursuing your passion or not.**

At the beginning of each day do you feel a sense of opportunity or a sense of dread?

Dreading going to work and the same routine over and over is absolute insanity and you have a choice to change this. Bring passion into your life and it will influence you more positively than you ever thought possible. Your passion will overflow into every part of your life and you will feel purpose. You will feel a fullness in life that you have either never felt before or that you have felt before and forgot you had the ability to feel it.

This is obviously something that I am extremely passionate about (excuse the pun) and something that has influenced my life.

I played a sport for years after I had lost the passion to play. I buried my passion so that I could please others. I buried my passion and did what I thought I was supposed to do because that is what the outside expectations were. I pursued a false passion on the field and suffered for years because of that decision. It fed into my alcohol abuse and created an edge in my personality that drove many people away. I am still paying for those decisions to this day.

All of that being said, things are improving day by day because I made the choice to pursue my true passion Off the Field. **I had to make a commitment to myself in order for things to get better and in order for me to have a chance to be the best version of me.**

That is my message.
It took me looking within to find my true passion and purpose.

It took me committing to myself and accepting everything I have done up until this point.

It took me committing to myself to take each day as an opportunity to improve.

It took me finding what it really was that I wanted to pursue which in turn showed me the true meaning of friendship and family.

People who care about you for you, just like you care about you for you, are the people you want around. They are the people who realize that you being the best you, and pursuing what you are passionate about, is what is really important. That is also what should be important to you regarding the people that are close to you in life. Support them for them and encourage them to pursue their passion. That is the ultimate gift you can give anyone.

This picture of pursuing your passion in life should inspire you to try to improve on a daily basis. I hope my examples and struggles have given you a chance to reflect on your experiences you have faced or are facing in your life. Realize the simplicity in which these concepts can be utilized.

It is all about taking single steps to get to where you want to go and achieve what you want to achieve.

At the end of the day it comes down to you. You have to answer to yourself at the end of each day for your actions and your words. You have to embrace the uncomfortable position of being different if you do not want to be average. You have to find out who the real you is and what you want to achieve.

Remember, You Are Going To Get Out Of Life What You Put Into It and You Have To Fight Through The Everyone To Become The Someone. Pursue Your Passion and You Will Find Your Purpose.

Chapter 11 Take Away

- **Find Your Passion**

- **ATTACK LIFE with PASSION and PURPOSE**

- **ANALYZE and ADJUST Constantly in LIFE**

- **Do NOT Go Through the Motions**

- **Be Smart and Consider Consequences When Making Life Adjustments**

- **Bring Passion Into Your Life as much as Possible**

- **COMMIT to YOURSELF**

- **EMBRACE the RESPONSIBILITY to BE the BEST YOU**

- **Support OTHER'S PASSIONS**

- **PURSUE YOUR PASSION**

Off The Field: Carving Your Own Path To Find Your Best Self

Note From The Author

If you have just completed reading the book, Thank You. In doing this, you have shown Self Discipline. You allocated time, held yourself accountable and got it done.

This journey of life that we are all on will be filled with ups and downs. We will have countless opportunities on a daily basis to improve, to learn and to be the elite version of ourselves. There are concepts in this book that will help you improve and help you get closer to your best life.

At the end of the day it all comes back to YOU. You have to hold yourself accountable and be honest with yourself.

Are you living your best life?

Is improvement a common part of your vocabulary and thought process?

Every single one of us knows the answers to these questions. We know our commitment level to ourselves and to whatever it is that we are currently doing.

My final word and concept to leave you with is education. There are a lot of amazing people out there that are living an elite life. There are a lot of amazing people out there that want to help others. Study these people as much as possible. This is not to say that you should copy them. You should learn as much as possible so that you can mold a lifestyle that works for you and makes you your best. Education never stops.

Be the elite person. Find out what you are capable of. Live life with passion and with purpose.

~ China McCarney